The Inspiration Blueprint
How To Design And Create Your Inspired Life

By BarbieTheWelder

Live INSPIRED!

Love,

BarbieTheWelder

The Inspiration Blueprint

Also Written By BarbieTheWelder

Horseshoe Crafts; More Than 30 Easy Projects You
Can Weld At Home

Contents

Dedication

Dedicated with love to my son Jamie. Without your support none of this would have been possible.

Dear Reader

I can only speak for myself and to the experiences and lessons I have learned from them. I share my truths here in hopes that if you're not already living an inspired life you can use this book as a blueprint to your own inspiration!

Those who know me know that I am not a person who candy-coats stuff! If you chose to live an inspired life you have lots of work ahead of you and you will have to be brutally honest with yourself and make decisions that will be difficult at times. I do promise if you choose to create a blueprint for inspiration and have the courage to make the necessary revisions to your current life you will be the happiest most authentic version of yourself!

I have lived uninspired and inspired lives. When I was living uninspired I was moderately happy, but something was missing, something felt off. There was no passion, no purpose, and no direction. My life involved going to work and making just enough to pay the bills to afford my crappy apartment in a crappy neighborhood that I hated. When I created my inspired life, the difference was like night and day! Even though it was the same life in the same neighborhood at first it was still better, brighter, and happier! Even though my environment didn't change at that time, my mind did. In 15 seconds I found direction, passion, and purpose!

My inspired life started in March of 2007 when I was sitting with family and friends in my crappy apartment watching the movie Cast Away starring Tom Hanks. At the beginning of the movie there was a woman who was welding a giant angel wing sculpture in her barn. It was a 15 second clip but it hit me like a wrecking ball and I spent the rest of the movie dreaming about being a metal sculptor and figuring out how I could make it happen as soon as humanly possible. Did Tom ever make it off the island? Who is this Wilson character you speak of? I missed the entire movie!

I am happy to say that I have since moved out of that crappy apartment and today I am living my life as a full-time world-renowned metal sculptor!

It didn't happen overnight, in fact from that moment till today it has been eleven years, but I can't even put into words, (great job Barbie, some author you are!) how rewarding and beautiful my life has become in that time! In those eleven years I have learned many lessons that I share with you here in The Inspiration Blueprint in hopes that you too will create your inspired life! As you design and create your blueprint please remember to build with love, be patient with yourself as you journey, learn, and grown because after all we are all human!

With love and gratitude,

Barbie

Be Unapologetically Authentic

"Be honest about what makes you happy and then align your life with those things."

-BarbieTheWelder

When I decided I was going to be a metal sculptor my husband and family were against the idea. I had no training in welding or art, no garage or workshop to weld and create art in, no machines or tools to weld and create art with, and to top it off our financial situation was dire at best. In my heart I knew that it was my soul mission to create sculpture and that I must find a way, anything less would be unacceptable. I worked and saved for nine months to get the $1,200 tuition to a local adult education program for welding. Even though everyone I cared about felt I was crazy and was making a mistake, my greatest desire was to be a metal sculptor and I unapologetically went after that dream.

Be unapologetically your authentic self! Being unapologetically your authentic self means living life in a way that is aligned with your dreams, goals, and desires, aligning your life with what makes you happy, everyone else be darned! Living an unapologetically authentic life does not mean being a jerk to someone who wants something for you that you don't want for yourself, it means not compromising or apologizing for what makes you happy, there is a difference.

Your first knee jerk reaction may be that this sounds selfish, but in all reality it's the opposite of selfish. Selfish is living a life based on what someone else wants that is not in alignment with what you want and giving your joy away because you aren't living life based on your dreams, goals, and desires, then feeling miserable and treating those closest to you like crap.

The harsh reality is we humans rarely do what truly brings us joy. We allow our families and society to dictate to us what makes us happy, whether it is a job, someone we date, or the clothing we ware. Many of us have allowed our own hopes, dreams, and desires to be put on the back burner or completely ignored just to please friends or family.

If you've been living your life for someone else for so long you may have lost your authentic self. Have no fear, it happens to everyone in their lives. We accept behavior that isn't acceptable, we say yes to people who ask for favors when we really want to say no, we work at jobs we hate or go to school for a career that is not of our choosing because someone close to us felt that is what is best for us. People in our lives don't do this maliciously, they just want what they FEEL is best for us. The problem is they are coming from their experiences in life and that colors their world differently from the world we see because of our experiences.

So how do you live your authentic life unapologetically? You need to know what your authentic life looks like, you need a picture, a blueprint!

Create Your Blueprint

"I saw in my mind what I desired my life to be and then I reverse engineered, worked backwards, until I knew each step I would need to take to get me there!"

-BarbieTheWelder

When I saw the woman in the movie welding those angel wings it gave me direction. For the first time in a long time I knew what I wanted my life to look like! I wanted to make sculptures like that woman was, I wanted to weld, bend, and cut metal to create something from nothing! I could think of nothing else! It spoke to my soul and stirred in me a deep desire.

In the beginning I didn't know that I had found the blueprint that created my inspired life. I knew what I wanted to spend my time doing, and it wasn't hauling scrap metal for pennies a pound and breaking my back just to unhappily scrape by like I had been doing for the last couple years.

Creating a blueprint gives you a clear picture of your sour mission! Having a blueprint and knowing exactly what you want your life to look like is the most powerful thing you can do for yourself! You can't get somewhere if you don't know where you want to go!

Some people, maybe you, already have their blueprint and are running down their dream. If so, LUCKY YOU, keep running it down!! Some people have their blueprints created but have ignored or crushed it way deep down inside because, parents, society, or whomever feels it's unpopular, unrealistic, or unachievable. If so, LUCKY YOU, it's go time baby!!

If you don't already have a clear vision of what you would like your life to look like, a blueprint, you need one. The rest of the book will be useless to you unless you complete this crucial step. If you already have a crystal-clear blueprint, I'm so proud of you, you're a rare bird!! If not, no worries, I've got your back! Let's get rare!!

How to get a crystal-clear blueprint of your perfect life.

Set aside time, whether it's an hour or a weekend, shut out any distractions, turn off your notifications on your phone, get a babysitter if you need one or wait until the kids are sleeping. For the best results your attention needs to be 100% focused on what you're doing.

Get a place to take notes whether it's your phone, a computer, or a notepad, a quiet space, and if you're anything like me, lots of coffee!

Think deeply and answer the following questions. It is of the utmost importance that you are specific and honest about what makes you the happiest, don't be swayed by what others want for you.

- What job/career would I do for free? The answer has to make your heart sing, has to excite you! No answer is wrong or too farfetched, but keep in mind that if you're 70 chances are you will not be able to play in the NFL, you could however still work in that arena! This is NOT about the job that would make your parents, friends, or neighbors happy, this is all about you and your happiness, everyone else be darned! If your answer makes your heart beep faster, (Yes, I said beep, that's the sound your heart makes on a heart monitor isn't it?) then you have found your heart's desire. If your answer doesn't make your heart beep faster, then keep working on this until it does.

- What kind of income would I love to have? (Come on now, just because you would happily do your job for free doesn't mean you are going to!) How much money would be ideal for you to make each year? (If your goal is $100,000 a year but being a busboy makes your heart beep faster you can have both, it's just a matter of problem solving how to do it! Passive income from the internet is a beautiful thing!)

- What do I want my relationships to look like? Think about your current relationships whether it be marriage or long-term relationship with a partner, if you have children your relationships with them, relationships with family members, friends, boss and coworkers. Write down how each

16

of these relationships would look if they were perfect. Would you be happier single or in a relationship? Does visiting your parents every day sound perfect or perfectly awful? Again, there are no right or wrong answers, just what makes you happy!

- What would my schedule look like if it was perfect? Does working 4 days a week sound appealing? Would you love to travel three months each year? Does being home every night with your family sound perfect, or how about being invited to the best parties? Think deeply about how you would like to spend your days?

- Where would I love to live? Again, everyone else be darned what city, town, or country would you love to live in?

- What kind of living space would make my heart sing? A tiny home, a cabin in the woods, a high-rise apartment in the city, a VW bus traveling the world?

- How do I want to spend my free time? Is there a cause you would love to volunteer for? Does being perched on a hilltop writing your memoirs sound intoxicating? Does going fishing, shopping, or skiing all day sound like perfection? How about sitting on your front porch with a dog and a shotgun? (My personal choice!)

Answering these questions honestly will give you the clarity you need to create your blueprint. These may be very easy for you to answer or very difficult. You may realize that you've been living someone else's blueprint, you may be in the wrong relationship, have the wrong job, or have been working towards a career that you are not passionate about. Don't be mad at yourself if this is the case, being mad won't change anything, the sooner you face the facts the sooner you can get yourself living life by your blueprint!

Occasionally blueprints need revisions, it's important to review these questions regularly. You may find what was important to you in the past has changed or you have moved away from your path. The sooner you realize you need to revise your blueprint the easier it will be for you to continue creating your inspired life!

The Inspiration Blueprint

Be Courageous

"I have been fearful many times in my life, but I find that my greatest growth has come each time that I act in spite of it."

-BarbieTheWelder

Once I realized that being a metal sculptor was my greatest desire it gave me a clear picture of what I wanted my life to look like, my blueprint. My family was on welfare, had no savings, and was living in the projects, however I didn't let that stop me. I made a definite decision (you could say I made a defiant decision) that I was going to go to school to learn how to weld so that I could be a metal sculptor. Everyone in my family was against me, against my decision, and didn't believe in me. They spouted every reason why I shouldn't, why I would fail, why my decision was wrong, how I was being selfish, and how my family would suffer if we had to save the money for school. I did it anyway. I was scared they were right but my fear of being wrong was only diminished by my fear of not following my soul mission. I had spent years not being truly happy and I figured worst case scenario I would try and fail, I already wasn't a metal sculptor, so I felt like I had nothing to lose and everything to gain!

Be courageous! Even if everyone is against you, if you feel a path is right for you stand your ground! Only you know what is right for you!

Now that you have your Inspiration Blueprint you might find that you need to revise your current blueprint. If you were perfectly honest with yourself answering your questions you might have found that you are in a relationship that you're unhappy with, have a job that you hate, or are living in a neighborhood you despise, or you might find that it's all the above like I did! Your mission, should you choose to accept, is to have the courage to change these things.

Being courageous is about doing what is right for you, not what is popular. At the end of the day we must be able to look ourselves in the mirror and feel good about who we are. Each time we stand up for what we believe in we build self-confidence, it's an empowering feeling! Be courageous and make yourself be heard, even if your voice trembles! Our greatest growth comes when we feel the fear and do it anyways!

The Inspiration Blueprint

Live To Learn

"I live to learn! I do what I lovingly refer to as information stacking, I deeply study several subjects and then combine them. This allows me to think and move in different worlds, be innovative and implement strategies that other entrepreneurs wouldn't think of."

-BarbieTheWelder

Just because I loved my welding class didn't mean I was any good at welding! During my time at school and the early years of my job at the custom fabrication shop I struggled to make the beautiful welds I saw seasoned welders make, and I made many mistakes in fabrication. Grinding out my crappy welds time and again was tough on my ego and it was frustrating when parts I created were rejected by quality control. The entire experience was humbling, but each time I made a mistake I was able to learn from it, whether it was something as simple as forgetting to turn on the gas before I started welding or something bigger like not reading blueprints correctly and making an entire pallet of parts wrong! Even though I felt like quitting at times I kept practicing and learning from my mistakes and over time my welding and fabrication skills improved.

Learning from our mistakes and successes, and the mistakes and successes of others is a powerful way to grow and improve!

Study yourself in a detached (let go of emotions and just look at the facts) manner and look for revisions you can make that will bring your life closer to your Inspiration Blueprint. Be honest when you see behaviors you are not happy with or things that you need to improve. Each time you find a revision that needs to be made you have three choices, you can waste time beating yourself up wallow in self-pity and make excuses, ignore it totally, or work to improve that area. When you choose to shut out the self-pity and excuses you are able to focus all your energy on improving. If you are used to wallowing and making excuses like I was it can be changed, it was one of my first revisions! I was a horrible welder and fabricator when I started out, but I chose to spend my energy improving because I was so excited about my blueprint I never even thought about wallowing and making excuses!

Frequently ask yourself these questions:

- What revisions can I make in my life to bring me closer to my Inspiration Blueprint?
- What revisions can I make to improve my home life?
- What revisions can I make to improve my job/career/entrepreneur life?
- What revisions can I make to make me better for the people around me?
- What revisions can I make that would make me happier?

Each time you make a mistake ask yourself:

- What can I learn from this?
- How can I grow from this situation?
- How can I make sure this never happens again?

The Inspiration Blueprint

Be Bold

"Making bold moves is necessary to create a life that you are proud of, but when you plan your bold moves they are much less daunting!"

-BarbieTheWelder

After five years of working at the custom fabrication shop I had fixed my credit, bought myself a motorcycle, a Jeep Wrangler, (my dream vehicle ever since I saw Daisy Duke step out of one!) 2 boats, (one for ponds and small lakes, and a bigger one for big water) bought a home, (for the garage) had purchased two welders, a plasma cutter, an air compressor, and some tools for my art studio (my one car garage). Life was good! I had been making metal art for a year at home, I loved my job, and my family was on my side and proud that I was a welder.

Every day after work and on the weekends, I worked in my garage creating metal art. Although I loved my job and the people I worked with the desire to create great metal sculptures was not satiated by working part time. It was time to make the move that I knew in my heart I would make before I even took the job, it was time to quit my job!

My parents freaked, (this is a giant understatement!) my friends freaked, and I put in my 1-month notice. I cashed in my 401k, had some money in a savings account, and the day before my last day I went to my bank and took out a personal loan (Yes ma'am I'm gainfully employed!).

Making changes in your relationships, living arrangements, or profession all take boldness, but they may be necessary to create the life you see in your blueprint. If you're involved in something you don't believe in or aren't standing up for something you do believe in, it's time to make a bold move. Have you always wanted to be a radio announcer but you're unhappily spending your days as a lawyer because your parents pushed you to be? Are you working at a 9-5 job when all you can dream about is working for yourself making widgets? When you boldly choose what is right for you over what everyone else feels is right for you

you are saying I deserve to be happy and what I want matters!

If you look at your Inspiration Blueprint and find that you have revisions to make that will take bold moves it's time to start planning! When people get to this point and realize the power they have in their lives to change their lives they want to jump right in and change everything now now now, but making successful bold moves requires planning and preparation. Want to quit your job to pursue your passion of being a singer, wonderful, plan for it. Want to leave your spouse because try as you may you can't find common ground, wonderful plan for it. The better you plan for your bold moves the easier your boldness will be.

When I planned to leave my secure job, I thought having six months of income in savings would be all I needed to see me through to success. HA! My ignorance was only exceeded by my ignorance! I was so blinded by my desire to create sculpture that I forgot about needing knowledge of art, business, branding, marketing, sales, website design, quoting, materials purchase, social media, photography, and the list goes on! Looking back, I'm stunned that I was able to succeed. I'm so grateful that I was ignorant because I never would have left my job otherwise, but because I did I've grown and learned considerably from it.

So how do you plan for bold moves, you think deeply! Set aside time, find yourself a quiet area, and grab a note book or way of taking notes. At the top write your bold move, and then below it list every possible thing that can go wrong when you make this bold move. (Yes, I know this seems negative, but wait there's more!) Your job is to have constant personal, financial, and legal anticipation, and then plan for it in advance! (In layman's terms, CYA!!!!) For each thing that you list that could go wrong I want you to write at least three solutions for it. Anticipating problems before you make your bold move will remove uncertainty and fear, prevent many problems from happening, and put you in a stronger position to succeed. When you plan like this it will save you from having to suffer like I did.

Never Give Up

"I didn't want to be a sculptor, I needed to be a sculptor."

-BarbieTheWelder

After quitting my job, I worked for six months in ignorant bliss before the bottom fell out. I had been putting in fourteen-hour days seven days a week creating art but had only sold a couple commissions, and by a couple I really mean only two! I was working three times as many hours in my shop as I had been when I was still full time at the fab shop, so the cost of running my shop was three times higher than I had anticipated. My savings had dwindled away so I sold my motorcycle, both boats, much of my hunting gear (not my guns), and my sons four-wheeler to continue creating art. I cried. Three months later I had $36 left in the bank and nothing left I would consider selling. Any rational person would have gone back to work at a nice secure job. I became depressed and cried a lot more.

We all face adversity and hardship in our lives. How you handle hardship will determine whether you will succeed or fail. Some people get the news that they have cancer and say I'm going to live, and they do, and others get the news and say I'm going to die, and they do. When you face adversity will you quit, or will you keep going?

I can't explain the fear that I felt when I saw that $36 in my bank account and realized that my dream, my burning desire to be a metal sculptor was not going to happen. The thought of my kids seeing me fail, the thought of me failing, was unacceptable. The idea of having to go and ask for my job back and not creating art was sickening to me. The idea of having everyone who didn't believe in me be right was downright offensive. Acquiring strength from all these fears I was able to pull myself up by my bootstraps and turn everything around. I didn't want to be a sculptor, I needed to be a sculptor. I needed to succeed as much as I needed to breathe.

I can't teach you how to never give up, I can only give you my experience. The only way you will never give up when you face massive adversity is to have an insatiable desire. This bears repeating. The only way you will never give up when you face massive adversity is to have an insatiable desire. A lukewarm desire will not pull you through when crap hits the fan.

The Inspiration Blueprint

Be Honest

"Facing the truth about my personal shortcomings as a business owner was the only reason I was able to move from failure to success."

-BarbieTheWelder

I sat down, thought deeply about what I needed to do to thrive as an artist, and made a list. The first thing on my list was to sell my art! No kidding! I'm not a stupid person but honestly this concept escaped me for a long time! I assumed that by making awesome art and posting a few crappy pictures on Facebook people would beat a path to my door. I was wrong!! I needed to learn how to actively sell my art. The second thing on my list was to use the power of social media to promote my business. The third thing on my list was to learn everything I could about running a business and being an entrepreneur. By thinking deeply and being honest about my shortcomings I was able to realize how I was failing and what I needed to do to change that. It was humbling for me to realize what a fool I'd been, but at the same time it was empowering because now I had the power to do something about it.

Just like trees and plants we need to grow to thrive! We grow by learning, and the more honest we are with ourselves about the areas we need improvement in, the faster we can grow, and the more inspired our lives will become! When we are honest about any shortcomings we have it gives us the power to change them!

These days I take an honest look at myself and my business monthly and ask myself the questions that are at the end of the Live To Learn chapter. This allows me to improve myself rapidly. By asking yourself these questions on a monthly basis you will move yourself through revisions quicker. Each revision you make brings you closer to the life you have designed for yourself in your Inspiration Blueprint.

Be Responsible

"It was my fault my business was failing. I could have claimed ignorance or played the blame game but doing so would have taken the power to change out of my hands."

-BarbieTheWelder

I found a local entrepreneur group and started attending monthly meetings, spent time everyday educating myself about running a business, learned how to promote my business online, and found events where I could set up and sell my art. I met and spent time with entrepreneurs at the shows I was attending, asked a ton of questions and learned everything I could, then went home and implemented what I learned. I voraciously read books and watched videos created by entrepreneurs I admired who freely shared their experience and advice. I had been working 14-hour days, I started working 16-18 hour days. Things started turning around for me.

The harsh reality is if our life is not exactly how we want it to be right now we only have one person to blame, ourselves. If you are in an abusive relationship it is not your partners fault, you choose to stay when you know that person is an abuser. If you are poor and unhappy it's your fault, you choose to not change. Our lives and situations are not our parents fault. We are not where we are because of our upbringing or because of some unfortunate situation that happened to us once upon a time, those things are excuses. Just look at people like Tony Robbins who made a choice to be responsible for his life and make changes so that he didn't have to live poor as an adult like he was raised to be as a child.

When I was honest about where I was failing as a business owner it gave me the power to do something about it. My first knee jerk reaction was embarrassment but my second was empowerment. Before I quit my job, I knew I was going to start a business as an artist and needed to depend on this business for my income, yet I never made the choice to educate myself in business or sales. I had screwed up massively and had lost a lot in the process, but now I had the power to do something about it.

Our greatest growth comes when we say, "I am responsible for this situation." When we choose to be responsible for our actions we give ourselves the power to make changes and can improve our situation. Saying, "I'm responsible," is not about wallowing in self-pity or being a martyr, it's about taking accountability for your current situation and saying, "I have the ability to change this." There is something very powerful about telling yourself, "I got me into this and I can get me out."

To create the life you designed in your Inspiration Blueprint you need to be responsible for where you are today and if revisions need to be made in your current situation you need to be honest with yourself and make plans to make the revisions necessary. To stay responsible in your life and keep the power to change in your hands ask yourself these questions;

- Am I happy with my current situation, job, schooling, relationship, friends, living arraignments?

- What choices can I make to change my situation?
- How can I educate myself so this situation never happens again?

Work Smart

"I laser focus all my energy on the two things that are most impactful to my business, creating epic sculptures and selling those sculptures."

-BarbieTheWelder

I started traveling to shows and events to sell my art and get my name out. All week long I would create art and then on the weekend I would cram myself, my son, two plastic folding tables, two chairs, and my sculptures into my Jeep Wrangler and we would go to craft shows and small fairs. As we traveled I was listening to audiobooks on business and selling and learning everything I could. Anytime I wasn't welding or driving I would read autobiographies about entrepreneurs and business books. At shows we slept in the Jeep because every penny I earned went to pay for other events, traveling to those events, and Spaghetti O's. During 2015 we traveled to 17 shows in New York and Pennsylvania. Long hours in the shop and on the road started paying off and at the end of 2015 I was able to trade my Jeep in for a truck (we had so much more room to sleep!)

At one show we attended I saw chainsaw sculptors creating their art live, saw the audience that gathered to watch, and decided I need to figure out how I can create sculptures live and gather my own crowd. In 2016 we traveled to 48 shows in 7 different states and I welded live in 4 of those states! In August of 2016 I was sitting at a show that was slow and I was bummed about all the time I spent sitting at events to sell, I missed creating art. I had been getting my name and art out, but I had less and less time to create, my business was improving but my sculpting skills weren't. I decided at that show that as of January 2017 I would not travel to sell my art, that between now and then I would learn how to sell it online. Events had been hit or miss, some did well, and some were awful. Depending on the event we set up at I was only able to reach 250-2500 people, online there are 3.6 billion people, that's billion with a B! It was a no brainer for me, learn how to sell art online. Selling online would give me the time in the shop to improve my skills and learn to create the sculptures I wanted to and give me the potential to reach billions of people versus the hundreds I was reaching.

Looking back, I had been working very hard, just not on what I feel was 100% the right things. When we are in a situation it is sometimes hard to see the entire situation, it's like being inside a house and being able to see the inside but not the outside, there's more to the picture. After not selling anything for a long time I went to one show, successfully sold $150 in art, and thought shows were the answer to making money.

Working smart means spending your precious time on earth doing what is most productive to get the results you want as efficiently as possible. If you are running a business, it means spending your time doing the things that are the most important for your business to thrive. If you want to be the best spouse or partner to someone it means spending your time working on improving yourself and not nagging or complaining. If you want to have a fantastic social media page it means studying how to do that, not scrolling through weldporn pictures for hours!

Just because you're busy doesn't mean you are being productive. Choose one area of your Inspiration Blueprint that you have been improving yourself in and ask yourself these questions about it;

- Is there a better or faster way to get the same result?
- Are there skills I can learn to make this easier?
- Has anyone done this before with better results, and how have they done it?
- Am I laser focused on what's important?

By asking yourself these questions regularly you can streamline your actions, get better results and be more productive in less time.

Be Patient

"Being an entrepreneur has taught me patience, growing both myself and my business into something I can be proud of has taken time."

-BarbieTheWelder

After that show in August 2016 I went home and started studying how to sell online. I had been selling art through Etsy, an online site like eBay but for artists, since November 2014 but now I really started promoting it. I improved my website and studied how to market through social media. When January 2017 rolled around I was ready for the online sales to pour in, wait for it, wait for it! They trickled in, seventeen sales to be exact, just enough to buy more spaghetti o's for the month and keep the lights on. I made twelve online sales in February, nine in March, and only four in April. I was scared I had made an awful mistake and I questioned my decision to sell online. I was spending time creating art, learning new sculpting techniques and improving my online skills, but I wasn't making much money. Although I was scared, I decided that I hadn't given myself enough time to make the transition from selling at events to selling online. I soldiered on and continued to improve myself in all areas that I saw weaknesses in and slowly my sales, income, and sculpting began to improve. I began to have some major wins! By August I had grown my social media presence large enough to attract a company to sponsor me, was making regular sales of mass produced welded art and few one of a kind sculptures, and had my first book (Horseshoe Crafts, 30 Projects You Can Weld At Home) published.

If you're a patient person, then huzzah! You're among the few! In todays society of one day shipping, and the seemingly overnight success of superstars and businesses, (we don't see the thousands of hours behind the success) we are conditioned to want everything right now.

As ironic as it is, learning patience takes time! When we decide to change our first instinct is not now, right now. We see this beautiful blueprint of our perfect inspired life and want it immediately.

We look at where we are and get frustrated and unhappy we are not where we want to be. When we are frustrated and unhappy about not being where we want to be our focus is on our feelings (internal) and not the actions (external) we can take to improve our situations. When we focus our time and attention on what we can do to improve our situation we move ourselves closer to our desired outcome, we become action based instead of reaction based (doing something about our situation instead of thinking about what we haven't done or all that needs to be done). As we work on what we can do right now in the present moment we move ourselves closer to our desired outcome and we see progress which removes the frustration. Patience comes as we stay in the present moment and work on what we can do right now.

It is important to be realistic about how much time it may take to make the changes you desire and make sure you are giving yourself the time necessary to make the changes. Having unrealistic expectations of your time will put unnecessary stress on yourself and make you feel unhappy and frustrated.

When you're feeling frustrated or unhappy about your situation take a few deep breaths and ask yourself these questions;

- Have I given myself the time necessary to make the changes I desire?
- What action can I take right now to improve my situation?

Patience takes practice but by being patient we show ourselves love and we give ourselves the room and time necessary to grow.

Embrace Change

"My greatest growth has come as a result of me making changes in spite of the fear I had felt at the time!" -BarbieTheWelder

Throughout 2017 I mass produced hot dog cookers and horseshoe art and created several one of a kind sculptures. I was finally succeeding financially but towards the end of the year I started feeling anxious whenever I had to create anything mass produced. Each time my supply ran out I had to force myself to go into the shop and make more and I would spend the entire time making them wishing I was creating the one of a kind sculptures I loved. Making mass produced art was paying the bills and feeding my belly, but it wasn't feeding my soul. I knew something needed to change so in November of 2017 I made the tough decision that after January 1, 2018 even though the mass-produced products were bringing in half my income I would no longer mass produce anything, all my sculptures from then on out would be the one of a kind sculptures that made my heart smile and fed my soul! Making the decision to go from mass producing art to creating one of a kind sculptures was scary, but I knew it was necessary to grow and evolve as an artist and to live my most inspired life!

Change means moving outside of our comfort zone and for most of us this causes stress and fear. As a reaction to stress and fear every human has a primitive fight or flight response, this used to protect us as we were hunting food with pointy sticks, but today, because it bypasses our rational brain, something as simple as thinking about quitting smoking or changing jobs can trigger it. When we first design our Inspiration Blueprint we get excited about living the life we have always wanted, but then the excitement fades and reality settles in, we see the changes we must make, and then our primitive fight or flight response kicks in. Our reaction may be, what was I thinking, I can't do this, or I could never make all the changes necessary to live a life like that, and we start making excuses and reasoning why we shouldn't change. These reactions are our natural fight or flight response trying to "protect us" from "danger" and keep us in our comfort zone where it is safe, warm, and fuzzy.

So how do we work through fear, stress, and our fight or flight response? (Notice I didn't say keep from being afraid or being stressed, I said working through fear and stress. We will always feel fear and stress to some degree, our goal is to learn to work through the stress and fear.) To work through stress and fear and provide a strong foundation for change we can redirect our attention and become solution focused by asking ourselves these questions;

- What are three positive things that will happen by making this change?
- What are negative consequences that may occur if I don't make this change?
- How will this change add to my happiness?
- What are some possible pitfalls I might face?
- For each pitfall what are three ways I can protect myself from the pitfall?

When we first designed our Inspiration Blueprint it was the picture of perfection, but as we grow and change our blueprint may need to be revised. We may find that as we make revisions and improve ourselves what was once something we felt would enhance our lives may not be the direction we want to take anymore, or that we may have something to offer in an arena we never thought of. Each time you need to make revisions simply refer back to the Create Your Blueprint chapter and answer the questions again. Ask yourself those questions regularly to keep yourself on the most direct path to happiness and inspiration.

Change can be scary, but our greatest growth comes when we feel the fear and act anyways!

Be Grateful

"It's of utmost importance that every day I think about what I have in my life that I am grateful for, even if the only thing that comes to mind that day is coffee."

-BarbieTheWelder

Through tens of thousands of hours of hard work and dedication to my Inspiration Blueprint I have created a life for myself and my family that exceeds my wildest dreams and expectations! Today I am a world-renowned metal sculptor who gets to choose what commissions I create, spend as much time with my family and friends as I want, travel when and where I want, work with amazing individuals and companies who are giving back to their communities and providing excellent products and services, and I have an incredible group of supporters and friends I have met through my social media platforms! What more can a girl ask for!!!

Even though I am living the amazing life I designed for myself I still have days where I feel frustrated, tired, or sad, because I'm human! There are times when I'm frustrated with someone for their lack of driving skills, when I misquote a commission and spend ten more hours than I had planned to create something, or for no reason at all I wake up feeling sad or lonely. At times like this I need to refocus my energy and think about what I'm grateful for instead of focusing on what is wrong or what I'm upset about. I know that no matter how good my life is things like this creep up on me, so I have made it easy on myself to refocus my energy by keeping an ongoing gratitude list. When I catch myself feeling down, frustrated, or angry I work to refocus my attention and think about the things that I'm grateful for. It's not always easy, yes sometimes it takes me a whole day before I catch myself being a crabby patty, but by focusing on what I'm grateful for versus focusing on why I'm frustrated allows me to shift my thinking away from negative and focus on the positive.

Negativity is dangerous, being negative can push everything good out of your life including family and friends. Complaining, blaming, anger, frustration, sadness, and loneliness, makes us and all the people around us feel bad. Being negative is like taking a magnifying glass and using it to focus the rays of the sun to burn something. The sun, when focused through the magnifying glass, becomes more intense and can do more damage in one area quickly. If the magnifying glass is focused on negativity then a small fire of negativity can quickly spread like wildfire and burn everything in its path. If we take that same magnifying glass and refocus it on what we are grateful for then our gratitude will spread like wildfire. What we think about and how we feel effects every aspect of our lives. By focusing on gratitude our thoughts are positive and that outlook affects our perspective on life and our physical health!

If you have been a negative person in the past no worries, just like any skill, being grateful can be learned! If you already focus on gratitude in most things, then huzzah! Keep that stuff up!

Using the following topics as a guide make a list of everything in your life that you are grateful for;

- Home
- Family
- Friends
- Vehicle(s)
- Food
- Personal characteristics
- Plants or trees
- Pets or animals
- Possessions you cherish
- Books, magazines, newspapers, or movies you love
- Celebrities you look up to
- Craftsmen, artists, or creators you admire

Keep a copy of this list in your phone, on your desk, on your bathroom mirror, in your car, anywhere you spend time, and constantly read it. Make it a habit to read it at least first thing in the morning and last thing at night. If you are a chronically negative person post it in every room in your house and read it ten times a day!

Just like anything we practice, being grateful becomes easier the more we work at it. It is physically impossible to be grateful and negative at the same time so by focusing on what we are grateful for we push out any negativity. To live the beautiful life you have designed in your Inspiration Blueprint practice and learn to bring gratitude into your life.

Give Back

"Having the ability to give back to my community through my sculpture has been one of the many unexpected blessings that occurred because of my journey." -BarbieTheWelder

When I first decided to be a metal sculptor my dream was to make art, but as my journey progressed my dream progressed along with it. It started when I was still traveling to shows selling my art, someone approached me for a donation to support a cause and even thought I couldn't afford to at that time I donated a small silverware sculpture. It was a small donation, but it made me feel good that something I had created with love would go to help someone! After that, even though I wasn't in a good place financially, every show I set up at I would look for a nonprofit that I could donate art to. Later, as my business grew more financially sound, I was able to donate more valuable pieces that would help more people. When I stopped traveling to shows I searched and found people locally who needed donations and have been able to support my community through my art. Now that my business has grown to where it doesn't need my constant attention I have been able to volunteer my time as well as my art. Giving back through my art and volunteering my time has been a beautiful side effect of becoming a metal sculptor. It wasn't even on my radar when I first started but as my journey progressed it was something that just manifested and now has become an integral part of my Inspiration Blueprint! It feels amazing to be able to give back and giving has blessed my life in so many ways!

Find a way to make a difference! There are so many brilliant causes out there, locally and worldwide! Find a cause or causes that you love and do all that you can to help them whether you give your time, money, or both! The more you give back the better you feel!

Have Fun

"I'm a big kid, it's like my brain is missing the thingy that tells you, ok you're an adult now and jumping on the bed is not what adults do!"

-BarbieTheWelder

I never figured out how to grow up, not that I ever tried! I still stomp in puddles, jump on beds, climb trees, and love to play in the mud! I laugh at myself when I trip over something or screw up my words when I'm talking, and I still think pull my finger is funny! It's like I was born missing the thingy that tells your brain ok you're an adult now and laughing at farts isn't appropriate. (I am laughing so hard right now I have tears coming out of my face at the fact that my book is the only inspiration book in the world with the word fart in it! Somebody call Guinness! You're welcome!) My body grew up, but I never stopped being a silly kid.

Although not having self-control when I saw the giant puddle in a parking lot and jumping in it accidently splashing my Dad right before we walked into a restaurant wasn't my finest moment, (sorry Dad!) I can say that my uncanny ability to embrace my inner child might actually be my superpower! My ability to laugh at myself when I make mistakes and find humor in any situation (I put the fun in funeral) has given me resiliency.

Somewhere along the line we got the misconception that we have to be serious all the time once we become adults, I say hogwash and poppycock! If you have lost your smile and sense of fun somewhere along the way, it's time to go back and find it! Stop taking life so seriously, no one gets out alive! Just because you're a grown up (or going to be a grown up) doesn't mean you have to be serious all the time.

Your greatest power lies in your ability to discover ways to embrace your inner child, be silly, and have fun! Think deeply into your childhood and make a list of all the things you really enjoyed! Here are a few examples from my list;

- Swinging
- Chalking on a sidewalk

- Wearing footie pajamas
- Stomping in mud puddles
- Climbing trees
- Building forts
- Jumping on the bed
- Playing kickball/capture the flag/dodgeball
- Riding bikes
- Making funny faces
- Believing in magic
- Playing in the creek/pond/lake
- Singing silly songs
- Believing in happily ever after

In creating your list O' fun you might find that you need to revisit your Inspiration Blueprint! You may find that entering or creating a career based on something that you find fun might be much more in alignment with what you value, and therefore much more inspiring! Love to play in the mud? How about a career as a monster truck driver! I'm willing to bet my lunch money you wouldn't dread going to work!

Finding ways to bring more laughter into your life will greatly enhance your life. Laughing reduces tension, brings oxygen into our brain, and relaxes us. Instead of listening to the news as you drive somewhere listen to your favorite comedian. Not only will the jokes make you laugh it's much harder to have road rage while you're laughing! Watching funny movies is another great way to bring laughter into your life, make a list and have a funny movie marathon!

We all have a different idea of what we find to be fun, but whatever way you choose, make it a priority to consistently bring more fun into your life!

No Regrets

"I have always done what I have felt was right for me, even if everyone else in my life didn't understand at the time." -BarbieTheWelder

I could only imagine how I would feel today if I had listened to everyone who told me being a metal sculptor was a silly dream! Making the decision to follow my dream, even though it wasn't popular at the time, was the best gift I ever gave myself. My journey has been a long and very difficult one at times, but it's one of the more rewarding things I have ever done, and I've had many opportunities because of it that I never expected!

I have faced several pivotal moments in my journey to become a metal sculptor that have shaped who I am today. By asking myself two simple questions each time I was faced with a decision I was able to build the life that I designed for myself in my Inspiration Blueprint and live with no regrets.

- Is this in align with my Inspiration Blueprint?
- How would my 100-year-old self feel if I did or didn't do this?

Life with no regrets is really that simple! Each time we face a decision we need to ask ourselves these two questions. If our decision is not in align with our Inspiration Blueprint, then it's not a good idea. If our 100-year-old self sitting on the porch with a dog and a shotgun would be disappointed that we never tried to be a metal sculptor, then we have to at least try!

A Message From Barbie

By choosing to design your Inspiration Blueprint and create an inspired life you are doing something that most people don't have the courage to do. Chances are your journey will be long and difficult, but I promise that if you choose this path and diligently work to make the revisions to your current life you will be the happiest most authentic version of yourself! The decisions you make as you design your Inspiration Blueprint may not be popular but being true to yourself is more important than a popularity contest. I have always been of the opinion that it's better to be hated for who we are than loved for someone we're not. Know your worth and how unique you are, and know the world needs your amazing self! Each time you make a decision that is in alignment with your goals, values, and happiness you are giving yourself and the world a gift!

Sometimes our road can be lonely, and we struggle to believe in ourselves so when the going gets tough and you need someone to be there for you who understands call on me, I will be there.

My email address is BarbieTheWelder@yahoo.com, you can reach out to me anytime for support! I also highly recommend you check out my beautiful friend Joshua Coburn who is living his inspired life as a devoted mentor and motivational speaker. Joshua understands the struggle of building an inspired life and will be quick to support you if you are feeling stuck, frustrated, or unmotivated. You can find out more about Joshua on his website www.JoshuaCoburn.com connect with him through his Instagram page @joshuacoburn or reach him by email at Joshuacoburn@mannersandmotivation.com

I am so proud of you for having the courage to build and create your Inspiration Blueprint and live happily ever after!

Barbie Biography

Through hard work, determination, and wherewithal, Barbie is living the life she designed and created for herself in her Inspiration Blueprint! After training for five years to learn the art of welding and fabrication and earning her Journeyman in sheet metal and iron plate, Barbie quit her job September 1, 2014 to pursue her greatest passion, metal sculpture. Although Barbie had extensive training from fellow welders and fabricators at the company she worked for, her art is completely self-taught. With her unparalleled sculpture design and artistry Barbie has quickly become a world-renowned metal sculptor and has created sculptures for exclusive clients in thirteen different countries.

Not only does Barbie love to create she also loves teaching. Her YouTube channel, BarbieTheWelder, which is viewed by subscribers in 53 countries, is a wealth of information for artists and entrepreneurs alike. In Barbie's easy-going style she shares step by step videos on how to create a wide variety of metal sculptures and sound entrepreneur advice. In her first book Horseshoe Crafts, Barbie takes you through thirty horseshoe welding projects with easy to follow instructions and tons of pictures. Barbie's latest passion project has been live streaming her sculpture design, problem solving, and creation process on Twitch, a livestreaming platform that has been mainly for gamers, and on YouTube, revolutionizing the art and metal sculpture worlds.

Barbie lives in Erin, NY where she continues to pursue her greatest passion, pouring her heart and soul into the metal that she sculpts into one of a kind sculptures for her clients all over the world!

Social Media

Website

www.BarbieTheWelder.com

Available Sculptures

www.Etsy.com/shop/BarbieTheWelder

Instagram

www.Instagram.com/BarbieTheWelder

www.Instagram.com/BarbieMetalSculpture

Facebook

www.Facebook.com/BarbieTheWelder

YouTube

www.Youtube.com/c/BarbieTheWelder